W0099715

Is It a Unicorn?

Is it a unicorn?

Yes, it is.

It's a unicorn.

Is it a rocket?

Yes, it is.

It's a rocket.

Is it a cupcake?

Yes, it is.

It's a cupcake.

Is it a zebra?

Yes, it is.

It's a zebra.

Is it a mouse?

Yes, it is.

It's a mouse.

Is it a ship?

Yes, it is.

It's a ship.

Is it a tiger?

No, it's not.

It's a cat.

Let's learn about Saint Patrick's Day.

March

Sunday	Monday	Tuesday	Wednesday	Thursday	Friday	Saturday
1	2	3	4	5	6	7
8	9	10	11	12	13	14
15	16	(17)	18	19	20	21
22	23	24	25	26	27	28
29	30	31				

Trace the word March
and circle the date.